Why Money Is Difficult To Make

ELIJAH O. OSENI

Copyright © 2022 Elijah Oseni

All rights reserved.

ISBN: 9798351625935

DEDICATION

This book is dedicated to everyone in the struggle trying to make ends meet.

CONTENTS

1   Chapter One   **Money** 1

2   Chapter Two   **Characteristics of Money**

3   Chapter Three   **Time Value of Money**

4   Chapter Four   **Who Can Make Money?**

5   Chapter Five   **Why Is It Difficult To Make Money?**

6   Chapter Six   **Attracting Money**

7   Chapter Seven   **Conclusion**

PREFACE

"Why money is difficult to make" was created as a result of research, education, and current events. The idea of money is prevalent and significant because it is a fundamental component of a source of livelihood.

Human reports, nevertheless, indicate that the sad story about it is that it's challenging to make. Although it may be simple for some, the goal of this book is to help readers understand why they have trouble making money.

CHAPTER ONE

MONEY

What Is Money?

Money has a single context and the most common and shortest definition of money, as it appears in dictionaries and Britannica such is "a commodity accepted by general consent as a medium of economic exchange". One could add to the above definition the following: "money is a medium of exchange that allows people to obtain what they need to live". When it comes as standard pieces of gold, silver, copper, nickel, etc., stamped by government authority and used as a medium of exchange and measure of value, it is called hard money; money however, may be any paper note issued by a government or an authorized bank and used in the same way; when appearing as bank notes, it is called paper money. Money is also used as a preferred method of valuation: the price of a commodity of some kind is typically expressed in a set number of units of currency; this is the accepted value of money, accepted by both the buyer and the seller because the conventional value can also be used to buy other goods or services. It is not always necessary to utilize a monetary unit chosen as a value measure widely. For instance, during the colonial era in America, the Spanish peso served as the recognised means of commerce while the British pound served as the benchmark of value.

Why Money Exists?

Money exists because it demonstrated its effectiveness in economies that were centrally managed. Transactions of goods and services as well as the ongoing specialization of production are made possible by the presence of money and its roles as a unit of account and a measure of value. Trade would take the form of a direct exchange of one good for another in a barter-based economy where money was not utilized, just as it did among prehistoric peoples. It was a horribly complicated system, and the so-called "double coincidence of wants" was its fundamental flaw: In order to exchange tomatoes for shoes, for example, a farmer selling tomatoes who also needs a pair of new shoes would need to find a shoemaker who wants to buy tomatoes as well as come to some sort of agreement on what the tomatoes for shoes exchange rate should be, of course, depending on the relative prices of these two products. While bartering is still common in some parts of the world, money is increasingly seen as a more practical form of exchange that allows for more economic transactions. In a money economy, a producer or owner of a commodity may sell it for money that may be used to pay for more goods and services, saving them the time and energy needed to locate a potential buyer. Money is viewed as a cornerstone of daily life in our modern economic society, and this perspective is highly effective because: - it is recognized as a unit of account; - it is a widely recognized form of exchange; - it is simple to divide; - it can be durable and stable in terms of value;

When Did Money Appear?

Around 2,500 BC, the earliest records of the usage of money are found in Lydia's ancient kingdom as well as in Mesopotamia. (According to some historical texts, the Chinese invented coinage around the second millennium BC.) Here, money took the place of the barter system, which led to a true explosion in the variety of products available for trade. The majority of non-economic uses for money involved either traditional forms of exchange or ancient ceremonial rites with their lavish showy adornment. Trade in kind steadily increased, and some items tended to be chosen over others, primarily due to their capabilities as exchange mediums: Others were easily transportable and had high value densities, while some were robust and practical to store. Such items became widely valued, were simple to exchange, and eventually were accepted as money. Prior to the invention of coins and paper money (banknotes/American English bills), early types of money were used for bartering things. For instance, in ancient Asia Minor, metal cylinders of various sizes, metal disks in Tibet, and limestone disks in the Yap Islands were the first exchange items used as forms of primitive money. Other examples include rice or various small tools in China, cowrie shells in India, cocoa beans in Central America, dog's teeth in Papua New Guinea, quartz pebbles in Ghana, or gambling counters in Hong Kong. These items, which were initially accepted for specific trade activities alone, eventually shown their rising popularity and tended to be used for various non-economic uses and general trading use, successfully supplanting barter in the process. China is the country that is currently most largely acknowledged as the origin of paper currency (about AD 800). It was common practice in many ancient cultures to have laws that stated their set norms and demanded restitution for crimes or payment2 for brides; this was done to make up for the loss of a daughter's services to the head of the family. Rulers levied taxes or demanded tribute from their people, and religious authorities also prescribed the payment of taxes or various types of sacrifice (or offerings). This is how money emerged from deeply ingrained practices in prehistoric societies. Different types of money have evolved from the so-called commodity money, such as rice, cattle, and cowrie shells, which replaced the previous barter system. Hard money is made of precious metals, particularly gold and silver bars and ingots,5 or coins. Token money is made of other metals, like copper. Paper money or soft money, also known as representative money, is the type of money used today, like the banknotes (Amer. Eng. bills). Forms of fake money such bank deposits, treasury bills, bills of exchange, and credits that could be transferred by check quickly followed them. Modern innovations like the credit card and the check (American English check) serve most, if not all, of the traditional purposes of money.

TWO

CHACTERISTICS OF MONEY

The initial currencies were pretty straightforward. Other nations used tobacco, wooden coins, and cotton warehouse receipts as forms of payment. The adaptability and universal acceptance of modern money were absent from these early types of money. For something to be used as money, it needs to have the following qualities:

• Robustness: Money should be able to withstand repeated use.

• Portability: Cash needs to be compact enough to fit easily in pockets, purses, or clothing.

• Divisibility: Profits must be divided into several parts. You ought should be able to exchange money. By having various units of money, goods of various values can be paid for, and change for larger units of money can be made. Barter, on the other hand, requires goods that are traded to be of equal value.

• Uniformity: Coins and bills of the same value must all have the same appearance. The value of money must be consistent, meaning that two $20 bills must be able to purchase the same item.

- Recognizable: Money must be simple to identify. Everybody is familiar with the appearance of a dollar bill, ten-dollar bill, or quarter. We should also be able to distinguish between real money and counterfeit money.

- Relative Scarcity: It must be challenging to produce money. We would be inundated with fake money if it were simple to produce money like any other item. Our currency consists of unique coins made of metal and paper that are challenging to replicate.

Additionally, money could not be common items that anyone may find on a beach, such as sand or clam shells. The items used to earn money must be rare or difficult to produce.

Types of Money and Supply

Money was one of the oldest use for precious (rare) metals like gold and silver. Coins made of gold and silver satisfy each of the six aforementioned criteria. Species or hard money is money that is created from gold or silver coins. We don't have enough gold or silver to use as money in a country with the size of the United States. We substitute paper money for species. People accept paper money as long as the government will accept it for tax payments and as long as merchants will accept it as payment for goods. Our country's money supply at one point was not permitted to exceed the dollar worth of its gold reserves. It's possible that our nation would have produced more goods and services than there was demand for. We wouldn't have had a very large supply of money in the United States unless we had found enormous new gold or silver mining sites. In the 1930s, America abandoned the gold standard, which involved backing its currency with gold. The government's response was to back our currency with the annual dollar value of all goods and services produced in the country. The gross domestic product is this number (GDP). The GDP, or the volume of goods and services produced in the United States annually, is now the unit of currency issued by the government.

THREE

TIME VALUE OF MONEY

The idea that money in the now is worth more than money in the future is known as the time value of money. The prospective earning capacity of the current currency in relation to future currency is what caused it (Chen, 2020). According to the following financial theory, money is worth more as soon as it is received. supposing that money can yield more interest. TVM is occasionally also referred to as present discounted value. The concept of sensible investors served as the foundation for TVM. According to the hypothesis, sensible investors prefer receiving funds in the now rather than the future since funds have the potential to appreciate in value over time.

Variables

Time value of money implicitly includes five variables. The first investment that one holds in his hands, or the starting amount, is the present value, or PV, variable. Second, future value is the interest that will accrue and grow over time. The third variable is the number of periods, which gives an investment timetable. The growth of money over time, typically expressed as a percentage, is known as the interest rate. The final component of the payment is a sequence of equal and even monetary flows.

Example

For instance, suppose an investor was given the option of getting XYZ amount either now or in the future. The present would be a better choice because it has greater value, advantages, and opportunity costs.

Importance of time value of money

For investors, the concept of time worth of money is crucial. The investors held the view that current cash is preferable to future cash promises. Cash on hand or in the present can be invested in the present and used to produce income or capital gains (Smith, 2020).

Future money will be worth less because of inflation, which will reduce its value. Thus, the common perception among investors that getting money now can have greater results and is more valuable than getting it later.

Compound interest

Aside from advantages a clear illustration of time as literal money is provided by time of value money. The idea goes that money's value might diminish over time. The idea is crucial since it aids in determining the value of assets and their returns over various time periods. Investors use the Time

Value of Money formula to assess a financial asset's current and future value. Compound interest rates and the average rate of return are calculated. Compound interest aids in capital gains and reinvestment.

Opportunity cost

Additionally, the opportunity costs related to time that is valued at money also play an important part. The opportunity cost is the chance lost to reach a better one.

Example

For instance, if one chooses to invest XYZ amount in a CD, they may be passing up the chance to invest it in a better option. Therefore, one can evaluate the future value of two options and steer them toward a better one by using the time value of money.

FOUR

WHO CAN MAKE MONEY?

Money has undoubtedly provided both people and animals with a means of subsistence in the world of the twenty-first century.

Why I included animals may be a mystery to you. Feed for animals is purchased with money and is necessary for their survival.

Additionally, we need money to feed ourselves, to develop and become great, to manage our enterprises and firms, to support our children's education, and to take care of our families.

In essence, we can see that money is needed in all facets of life. Who among us is devoid of life? Absolutely no one!

FROM A CHILD'S PERSPECTIVE

As a child from age 0-18, there are only little ideas about making money one can have. This is as a result of child's inexposure to the real world, yet. However, it is stated that children from a poor background, if hardworking, starts making money around the age of 18.

When a child attain the age of 18, it is helpful that he starts thinking about making money by himself. This is a bitter truth this generation cannot afford to tell us. The parents owe a share of this duty, too.

FROM A REAL LIFE PERSPECTIVE

When I was younger, I was affected by some odd beliefs. I know most people were hypnotized with such beliefs, too. I was taught never to chase money. It was taken out from been a priority to life. "Just do well and be a good boy." they would say.

But as I grew up, I began to think about my life. "If I don't make money, how would I get to do with the issues of life?"

My needs were countless as the sands of the sea while my parents could only afford little out of my countless needs. Then, I knew I had to dissolve the thought and beliefs that has found its root in me. I had to learn how to make money by myself with the help of God.

As money is important in the issues of life, everyone who has life has to make money. You want to live a valuable and worthy life, make more money. As stated earlier, what we've come to live our lives for, needs money to be executed. Achievements require money.

Say to yourself, "I will make more money."

So, as far as money is important in the issues of life, everyone who exists at all should and must be able to make money.

FIVE

WHY IS IT DIFFICULT TO GET MONEY?

Payments and market-making are the two primary purposes of monetary systems. These form the cornerstones of what is known as the money view.

People come to the study of money with a variety of barriers, and it is important to recognize the requirement of bringing these barriers to consciousness as part of the learning process. However, a guess that 90% of money disputes have their roots in these unacknowledged walls is essentially pointless. But that is a topic for another time. What is known as the "alchemy of banking" is the first and biggest hurdle. Banks build their balance sheets on both sides simultaneously when they issue loans by generating deposits. This procedure seems to go against what one would expect a loan to mean—I can only lend you a bicycle if I already own a bicycle. Furthermore, it appears to violate the fundamental tenet of basic economics, which states that "there is no such thing as a free lunch." I steadfastly maintain that an IOU swap is the core of banking in the face of overwhelming opposition.

The second obstacle is "essential hybridity". While we typically aren't aware of this because bank deposits and central bank currency trade at par, money is made up of both private and public components. Similar to private bankers' banks, central banks are a mix of public government banks and private bankers' banks, with the proportions varying over time with financial progress and state requirements (such as war). However, it seems that it is difficult to recognize this fact of hybridity, mostly since it goes against political sense. According to Knapp and Menger, idealizations of pure public money appeal to the left while idealizations of pure private money appeal to the right, making the actual system appear to be tainted by unauthorized expansion to everyone.

Thirdly, despite the fact that they trade at par, there is a "inherent hierarchy" that makes central bank money superior than private bank money. To fulfill our obligations to pay, you and I use bank money, but banks also use central bank money, and central banks also use world reserve money. Because it violates our sense of fairness as between states—the Westphalian idea of equal sovereignty—hierarchy seems to be difficult to accept. It also offends our sense of fairness as it relates to market actors within states, which is significant for economics. A trained economist's natural aversion to hierarchies, monopolies, and other non-market forms of allocation stems from their sound.

What Hawtrey referred to as "the inherent instability of credit" is the fourth barrier. Despite the fact that promises to pay are made and accepted today, it is inevitable that the future they refer to will be different from what was anticipated when the promises were made. More importantly, all credit—bank and non—seems to be susceptible to some sort of positive feedback loop because, as more people share the same perspective of the potential future, the value of promises to pay in that potential future rises, making overpromising simple—if not inevitable.

We have a particularly difficult time accepting this fact of inherent instability because it is at the core of our existential predicament. Even if we don't know what the future holds, we must act as if we do. In fact, the fabric of the society in which we exist is created by the promises we make to one another to fulfill in various ways in the future. Credit is the same way, as is marriage. Financial instability poses a threat to this fabric and perhaps contributes to its unraveling as one set of promises that are broken undermines another. As economists, we adhere to ideas about equilibrium, such as intertemporal equilibrium, that have the consoling quality of removing instability, but the psychological comfort that results comes at the cost of abstraction from a key aspect of the actual system in which we live.

According to me, these are the four fundamental obstacles to comprehending. The main issue we face is that these four hurdles are made extremely challenging to overcome by the existing institutional fact of financial globalization. We are confused by so-called shadow banking, which I define as "money market funding of capital market loans" and believe to be the key institutional form of banking for financial globalization. Our intuition is based on the cozy but antiquated picture of Jimmy Stewart community banking. We long for a time when instability, hierarchies, hybridity, and alchemy appeared to be under acceptable social control. A stable ratio between public and private money was once promised by the "money multiplier," but no longer.

Money problems are never easy, and they are getting worse. However, the real challenge is not with the complexity of the universe, but with ourselves and our ingrained ways of thinking.

Here, we'll look at some of the most typical monetary errors that frequently result in severe financial difficulties. Even if you are already in financial trouble, avoiding these errors may be the difference between life and death.

WHY MONEY IS DIFFICULT TO MAKE

1. Excessive and Frivolous Spending

Large sums of money are sometimes lost one dollar at a time. When you order that pay-per-view movie, go out to dinner, or buy that double-mocha coffee, it might not seem like a huge issue, but everything adds up.

Spending just $25 a week on eating out costs you $1,300 year, which might be used to cover numerous additional credit card, auto, or other payments. Avoiding this error is crucial if you're struggling financially; after all, if you're just a few dollars from foreclosure or bankruptcy, every penny will matter more than before.

2. Never-Ending Payments

Do you really need those things for which you continue to make monthly payments year after year? Cable television, music services, and upscale gym memberships are a few examples of things that might make you spend continuously while leaving you with little in return. Living a leaner lifestyle can help you increase your savings when money is tight or you just wish to save more. This will protect you from financial difficulty.

3. Living on Borrowed Money

Using credit cards to pay for necessities has become rather typical. But even if more and more consumers are willing to pay double-digit interest rates on groceries, gas, and a variety of other products that are gone before the bill is fully paid, doing so is not a prudent financial decision. The cost of the things that are charged is significantly increased by credit card interest rates. Occasionally, using credit may result in you spending more than you make.

4. Buying a New Car

Even though only a small percentage of consumers can afford to pay in cash, millions of new cars are sold each year. However, being unable to pay cash for a new car can also indicate that you cannot afford it. After all, having the money to make the payment is not the same as having the money to buy the car.

Additionally, by taking out a loan to acquire a car, the buyer is paying interest on a depreciating asset, which enlarges the gap between the car's worth and the amount paid for it. Even worse, a large number of people trade in their cars every two to three years, losing money each time.

A person may occasionally be forced to obtain a loan in order to purchase a vehicle, but how many people actually require a large SUV? Such cars cost a lot to acquire, insure, and fuel. Unless you need an SUV to make a living or you tow a boat or trailer, buying one might be costly.

Consider purchasing a car that uses less gas, is less expensive to insure, and requires less maintenance if you need to buy one and/or borrow money to do so. Because cars are expensive, if you purchase more than you need, you can be wasting money that could have been saved or applied to debt repayment.

5. Spending Too Much on Your House

Bigger doesn't always mean better when purchasing a home. A 6,000-square-foot home will cost more in taxes, maintenance, and utilities unless you have a large family. Are you truly willing to make such a big, sustained dent in your monthly spending?

6. Using Home Equity Like a Piggy Bank

Giving someone else ownership of your home by refinancing and withdrawing money from it. Refinancing might make sense in some circumstances. if you can refinance and pay off debt with a higher interest rate, or if you can cut your rate.

But you can also open a home equity line of credit as a different option (HELOC). This enables you to effectively use your home's equity as a credit card. This can need paying extra interest just to use your home equity line of credit.

7. Living Paycheck to Paycheck

The personal savings rate for American households in June 2021 was 9.4%. 2 Many families may be living paycheck to paycheck, so if you are unprepared, an unexpected issue could quickly turn into a catastrophe.

People find themselves in a hazardous situation where they need every dollar they make and one missed payment would be terrible as a result of their cumulative expenditures. You do not want to be in this situation when an economic downturn occurs. You'll have very few choices if this occurs.

Keep three months' worth of spending in an account that is easy to access, according to several financial advisors. Your funds could be depleted by a job loss or economic developments, which would put you in a cycle of debt repayment. It might be the difference between keeping or losing your house if you have a three-month cushion.

8. Not Investing in Retirement

You might never be able to stop working if you do not put your money to work for you in the markets or through other investments that generate income. For a comfortable retirement, making monthly contributions to designated retirement accounts is crucial.

Utilize your employer-sponsored retirement plan and/or tax-deferred retirement savings. Know how long it will take for your investments to grow and how much risk you can take. If feasible, seek the advice of a seasoned financial counselor to match this with your objectives.

9. Paying Off Debt With Savings

If your debt is costing you 19% of your income but your retirement account is earning 7%, you might believe that switching the retirement for the debt will result in you pocketing the difference. But it's not quite that easy.

It is quite difficult to repay those retirement savings, and you risk being charged exorbitant costs, in addition to losing the benefit of compounding. Borrowing from your retirement account can be an option if you approach it in the proper way, but even the most diligent planners struggle to put money aside to rebuild these funds.

The urgency to repay the debt typically disappears once it has been paid off. You might get back into debt since it will be very tempting to keep spending at the same rate. If you want to pay off your debt with savings, you must continue to live as though you still owe your retirement fund money.

10. Not Having a Plan

Your financial future is dependent on the current situation. Setting aside two hours a week for your finances is impossible when people spend countless hours watching TV or surfing through social media. You must be aware of your destination. Make time for financial planning a top priority.

The Bottom Line

Start keeping an eye on the minor expenses that add up quickly to avoid the risks of overspending, then go on to keeping an eye on the larger expenses. Consider your options carefully before adding any more debt to your list of obligations, and remember that just because you can make a payment doesn't mean you can afford the item. Finally, prioritize saving a portion of your income each month and taking the time to create a solid financial plan.

SIX

ATTRACTING MONEY

Attracting Money Is Easier Than You Think

You've come to the correct place if you're looking for advice on how to attract money into your life.

How To Attract Money: Key Takeaways

First and foremost, attracting money begins in the mind. You must be financially savvy and have a positive outlook.

Additionally, you need to evaluate your financial situation honestly. And create a vision for what getting more money means for your future.

Finally, take the appropriate steps to increase your income. And be careful with your money.

We have derived our list of 15 suggestions for attracting money from these four crucial lessons.

1. To Attract Money, Have A Positive Attitude

Keep a positive attitude. Consider the positive side of things. Avoid focusing on the bad. When it comes to money, say positively to yourself.

Being upbeat will help you meet better people to associate with. And those better individuals will support you on your path to financial abundance.

Practice Positive Self-Talk

Just now, I brought up positive self-talk. What is that exactly?

Positive self-talk attempts to extract positive outcomes from bad situations or blunders. to support your efforts to improve, advance, or simply keep going.

You can find hidden optimism through the process of practicing positive self-talk. Moreover, the joy and the hope in each given circumstance.

Last but not least, have confidence in yourself. and what you want to achieve financially.

This is necessary to use the law of attraction to attract money. Who will believe if you don't?

2. Create A Productive Money Mindset

Your financial mindset describes how you approach money. You also need to concentrate on having the optimistic view of money we just discussed.

You must have confidence in your financial abilities. So you can increase your income. And put aside more of your earnings.

Think about wealth and money in a good light.

Politicians and the media occasionally demonize wealthy individuals.

Actually, the majority of those who are successful in acquiring money nowadays are honest, industrious individuals.

Having money is not a bad thing. or making an effort to seek additional funding. Don't think that way, then.

3. Knowing How To Attract Money Means Stopping Worry

WHY MONEY IS DIFFICULT TO MAKE

My experiences show that worrying is useless. Money problems can lead to stress in our life and worry.

We can become weakened by stress and concern. It might lead to health problems. We may become paralyzed and be prevented from seeking financial success at home or at work.

Therefore, it's crucial to appropriately handle stress.

I am all too aware of this. I have a fairly high stress level. I have had times in my life when stress nearly rendered me incapacitated.

Recognize that the majority of our worries never come to pass. When you are next experiencing financial hardship, consider your financial thinking.

Start by shifting your focus to a more encouraging concept. Because it's likely that none of your worries will materialize.

Additionally, take steps to allay your anxiety. Is there anything you can do about the problem you're thinking about? If so, then go ahead and do it.

You must manage your concern and tension if you want to learn how to attract money spiritually. You'll find your inner power and resolve by doing this.

Okay, let's go on. Our first major section of takeout is now complete. How to use mental power to attract money. Keep in mind that everything begins between your ears. We are now prepared to examine the second major component of this subject.

That is, being aware of how things stand in terms of quickly drawing money. Additionally throughout the long term.

4. Face The Facts & Make An Honest Assessment About Your Money Status

Get your financial facts together.

How much money do you have? What you spend your money on and where you spend it.

To evaluate your present financial situation, a free online tool like Personal Capital is an excellent resource. And take good care of your finances.

Are you an investor? So, what are they and are they the best investments to help you reach your financial objectives?

Therefore, take some time to familiarize yourself with your finances. Make a space where you may concentrate on your money at home to attract money.

The ideal solution is a home office. However, you can put it wherever you like. so long as you have access to your financial data.

5. To Attract Money Focus On Abundance & Be Grateful

Your knowledge of your existing financial situation has improved as a result. So, think of your possessions as abundance. Don't stress about what you lack.

This statement comes to mind whenever I'm feeling depressed about something. "I had the blues since I had no shoes until I encountered a man who had no feet on the street," said the man.

Be appreciative of what you have. And don't focus on the things you lack. A mindset of abundance will help you succeed.

Keep in mind that many individuals are less fortunate than you.

6. Share What You Have

WHY MONEY IS DIFFICULT TO MAKE

If helping others or donating to charities is important to you, don't forget to do so. One of the many effective wealth affirmations is giving.

I'm not a fan of donating cash. not yet, at least. However, some people firmly believe in it when it comes to attracting cash.

Perhaps your present financial situation makes it impossible for you to make a charitable donation. I comprehend.

However, giving doesn't always have to be financial.

It might be as easy as this. Put a smile on your face and let the world know it. Act kindly toward a neighbor or a friend.

You get back twice as much as you give, as my mother used to say. My mum was also always correct. That's what she told me, at least.

Okay. That addresses the second important aspect in our effort to draw funding. That is evaluating how you are right now.

Understand your present financial status before anything else. Take an abundance-oriented approach to that scenario as well. Last but not least, be kind to yourself and others.

The third crucial aspect in raising your vibration to attract money is the next to be discussed. Your future state is what it's deciding.

7. Make A Study Of Wealth To Attract Money

Wealth: What is it? How much cash do you require?

How do those who are effective at attracting money approach the process?

These are all crucial inquiries. Here at Dividends Diversify, we have a ton of resources on money, wealth, and increasing wealth.

I invite you to read any or all of the articles regarding accumulating wealth.

However, I'll highlight one so you don't feel overpowered. I've read and evaluated a book called Everyday Millionaires for you.

The book is chock-full of anecdotes from real life. Stories about the ascent to millionairedom of common individuals like you and me.

Define riches. Well, if you don't, how will you know what financial success looks like?

You can have the wrong ideas about how to acquire wealth.

The following phase in the process of how to attract money follows from that. It's deciding how you'll feel in the future.

8. You Must Visualize Money To Attract Money

Define riches. Well, how else are you going to know what achieving financial success looks like?

You can have the incorrect perceptions on how to amass cash.

That leads to the next step in the process of attracting funding. It involves choosing how you'll feel later on.

Attract money into your life by having your goal in mind. If you can imagine it, think large and have faith in it. After that, you can succeed.

Because of this, our first move was to educate ourselves about wealth. You must comprehend wealth building in order to create your vision.

A Narrative About Imagining Success & Money

I'll sum it up with a quote I recall hearing from a former boss of mine.

Joe was his name.

WHY MONEY IS DIFFICULT TO MAKE

Joe has just turned 70. In his 60s, he retired, but he detested retirement and went back to work.

Joe and I were in charge of creating a new business unit for our company at the time. Joe once told the workers at a group meeting to "Think big" since "we are only limited by our thoughts." And that saying is true for both me and you. The only thing limiting us is what we think when it comes to having a large financial mindset.

Heed Joe's counsel. Dream large, reflect on the future, and create your ideal scenario for financial achievement. Don't let your thoughts confine you.

Inquire within. How will your life change once you've succeeded in attracting money?

WHY MONEY IS DIFFICULT TO MAKE

A Quick Recap On Our Status Of Attracting Money

The fourth and final major area to obtain funding is now prepared. Because the majority of what we have talked about so far is conceptual.

We started by cultivating a helpful financial mindset.

In addition, I asked you to evaluate your financial situation right now.

You have finally researched wealth. and established the details of your financial objective.

But now we are prepared for more tactical moves. Why do I say that?

Well, there are really just two ways to increase your financial flow.

First, increase your income. Moreover, we should be more frugal with our resources.

with your current situation in hand. further financial objectives. Now that you're prepared, take these additional steps to generate a wealth of money.

9. To Attract Money Put Yourself "Out There"

To some extent, rejection and failure are fears we all share. However, you are unable to protect yourself from those things. Risk-taking comes with failure and rejection.

Don't fear failure. Embrace it.

The proverb "when one door closes, another one will open" is one that I appreciate. It certainly seems to be the case, in my opinion.

Don't run from your profession, whatever it may be. Or, as I like to say, "Put yourself out there." Additionally, present a favorable image of yourself.

Search for the following chance to increase your earnings.

Work harder at what you do, if necessary. by setting yourself up for a promotion. or obtaining a different, higher-paying career.

Your earning potential should be maximized. Even a small amount of side income may be beneficial.

10. Think In Terms Of Adding Value, Not Time

It's crucial to put in the effort and time. Don't misunderstand me here.

But if you're trying to attract money and you don't want to exchange time for money; whatever it is that you do for a living, you should consider how you may add value to it.

Consider how you can contribute to the success of your employer, your client, or your supervisor. That is how value is delivered.

Even a menial minimum wage job can be used to fund this. Here's an illustration.

I used to work at a restaurant and bakery that was situated on a 15-acre property while I was in high school and college. With gratuities from serving customers, it was a job paying the minimum wage.

I kept taking on more responsibilities gradually but steadily.

I took care of the grounds' landscaping. For major events and wedding receptions, I cleared tables, waited on tables, served beverages, and conducted setup.

Finally, I assisted with food preparation, dishwashing, and cleanup when the kitchen was understaffed.

In other words, I contributed greatly to the operation. The owner, who was my boss, constantly had things for me to do. Why?

I constantly sought out opportunities to bring value. and improve how the business is operated. Change it for the better.

I didn't feel hesitant to "throw myself out there." Doing the right thing the right way while adding value. Long-term, that is what pays out handsomely.

Consider how you can accomplish this in your environment. Only your imagination and attitude can hold you back.

11. Make Continuous Self-Improvement A Priority.

Continuous improvement is almost always a wise use of time and resources. Whether it through literature, training, certificates, or work experience.

Just make sure your self-investment is consistent with your primary areas of concentration for earning income.

Be better now than you were yesterday and better tomorrow than you were, as the saying goes.

The spending aspect of drawing money into your life is what we need to discuss next.

12. Spend In Alignment With Your Values

Determine your personal values. Travel, a lovely residence, delectable food, or live entertainment top the list, don't they?

I'm not sure what the issue is for you.

What you value may also alter over time. In my case, yes. Both earning money and spending it on things you value are crucial.

Spend money on the things you value, whatever what it may be. Likewise, stop spending money on other things in your life. Save a little more money however you can.

13. Attracting Money Is Easier When You Become A Minimalist

Just keep what you really must have and use. Reduce your spending by simplifying and streamlining your finances.

Purchase what you want and need. But resist the urge to consume simply because others are.

I like to say, "minimize your finances to maximize your money," even though it is somewhat contradictory.

14. Reward Yourself

Recognize and appreciate your small victories along the way.

SEVEN

CONCLUSION

Everyone should be able to identify compelling ideas about the purpose of this book after mentioning various aspects of money-making challenges and the reasons why it's difficult to generate money.

This book is filled with teachings that can only be discovered by someone who is paying close attention and has acute senses. For readers of all ages, young and old, it is a book that teaches and informs.

www.ingramcontent.com/pod-product-compliance
Lightning Source LLC
Chambersburg PA
CBHW050315220526
45465CB00005B/2007